THE WORLD CUP

by Tyler Omoth

CAPSTONE PRESS
a capstone imprint

Capstone Captivate is published by Capstone Press, an imprint of Capstone.
1710 Roe Crest Drive
North Mankato, Minnesota 56003
www.capstonepub.com

Copyright © 2020 by Capstone. All rights reserved. No part of this publication may be reproduced in whole or in part, or stored in a retrieval system, or transmitted in any form or by any means, electronic, mechanical, photocopying, recording, or otherwise, without written permission of the publisher.

Library of Congress Cataloging-in-Publication Data is available on the Library of Congress website.
ISBN 978-1-5435-9192-7 (hardcover)
ISBN 978-1-4966-5782-4 (paperback)
ISBN 978-1-5435-9199-6 (eBook PDF)

Summary:
Discover the legendary players, thrilling games, and long history of the World Cup.

Image Credits
Alamy: PA Images, 29; Getty Images: Bob Thomas, 23, Tommy Cheng, 13, 20; Newscom: AFLO/Juha Tamminen, 16, dpa/picture-alliance, 15, EMPICS, 8, 9 (top), Icon SMI/DPPI, 19, Photoshot/Talking Sport, 7 (left), ZUMA Press/Andrew Chin, 26, ZUMA Press/Pa, 7 (right), ZUMA Press/Richard Sellers, cover, ZUMA Press/Steven Limentani, 5; Shutterstock: A.RICARDO, 11, EFKS, 1, Jose Breton-Pics Action, 21, Lawkeeper, 9 (bottom), Leonard Zhukovsky, 10, Romain Biard, 24, skynetphoto, 17

Design Elements: Shutterstock

Editorial Credits
Editor: Gena Chester; Designer: Sarah Bennett; Media Researcher: Eric Gohl; Premedia Specialist: Spencer Rosio

All internet sites appearing in back matter were available and accurate when this book was sent to press.

Printed and bound in the USA.
PA99

Table of Contents

INTRODUCTION
The Kicking Kid 4

CHAPTER 1
History of the World Cup 6

CHAPTER 2
Great Teams 14

CHAPTER 3
Amazing Plays 22

Glossary 30
Read More 31
Internet Sites 31
Index 32

Glossary terms are **bold** on first use.

INTRODUCTION

The Kicking Kid

It was late in the game during the 2018 World Cup final. France was leading Croatia 3–1. France's Lucas Hernandez sprinted down the left side of the field. He passed the ball to teammate Kylian Mbappé. The 19-year-old star faked right and then pulled back. Mbappé kicked the ball left and into the net from 25 yards (23 meters) out. The crowd erupted into cheers. France went on to win the World Cup, and Mbappé won the Best Young Player of the World Cup award.

Mbappé was the fifth teenager to score a goal in the World Cup. His moment came 60 years after Pelé scored for Brazil in 1958.

CHAPTER 1

History of the World Cup

Soccer was extremely popular in Europe in the early 1900s. In 1904, seven European countries with soccer **associations** created the Fédération Internationale de Football Association (FIFA). FIFA allowed the best teams from France, Belgium, Denmark, the Netherlands, Spain, Sweden, and Switzerland to play against each other. Ten years later, teams from South America and North America had joined the **league**.

Fast Fact!

In 1966, the World Cup trophy went missing. Seven days later, a dog named Pickles barked and jumped around a parked car in London. His owner looked inside and spotted the stolen trophy!

Pickles discovered the stolen trophy on his evening walk with owner David Corbett.

From 1930 to 1970, winners of the World Cup were awarded the Jules Rimet trophy (left). Since 1974, teams have received the FIFA World Cup trophy.

By the 1920s, the leaders of FIFA saw the popularity of soccer in the Summer Olympics. They wanted their own championship tournament. They started the FIFA World Cup. The Cup was held every four years. On July 13, 1930, the first men's World Cup opened in Montevideo, Uruguay. There were 13 teams competing. Today, over 200 teams compete in tournaments to **qualify** for the World Cup. The best 32 teams move on to compete on the field for the World Cup.

Argentina's goalkeeper, Juan Bolasso, (left) misses the ball. This was Uruguay's fourth goal in the 1930 World Cup final. Uruguay beat Argentina 4–2.

Uruguay played Argentina at the Estadio Centenario stadium in the 1930 World Cup final.

Most World Cup Finals Championships

Men's	Women's
Brazil ✪✪✪✪✪	United States ✪✪✪✪
Italy ✪✪✪✪	Germany ✪✪
West Germany ✪✪✪✪	Norway ✪
Uruguay ✪✪	Japan ✪

Thirty-two **seeded** teams make up the first round, or group stage. They are split into eight groups of four. Every team plays at least three games within the group. Three points are given for a victory. One point is given for a tie. A loss gets no points. The two teams with the most points in each group move to the next round. It's called the knockout stage. The top teams from each group play the second-place team from another group. The winners of those games move to round three. The losers are knocked out. This cycle repeats until there are only two teams left. They play in the World Cup finals game.

Star Effort

Teams that have won the World Cup finals get a star. Players wear one star above their team's crest on their jerseys for each of their titles. Brazil's men's team has five stars, the most out of all teams, because Brazil has won the World Cup five times. The U.S. women's team has four stars.

With their 2019 World Cup win, the U.S. women's team will add another star to their jersey.

France celebrates its win against Croatia at the 2018 World Cup.

In 1991, FIFA introduced the FIFA Women's World Cup. The first Women's World Cup was played in Guangdong, China. Ma Li was a defender on the Chinese team. She was the first player to score a goal in Women's World Cup history. Twelve teams competed. The United States won the title.

Despite the smaller number of teams, the basic setup was the same as the men's World Cup. In 1999, the Women's World Cup grew to 16 teams. In 2015, there were 24 teams. The tournament is played in a different location every four years—just like the men's tournament. But while the men play on even-numbered years, the women play on odd-numbered years.

FAST FACT!

In 2018, 32 teams tried to qualify for the 2019 FIFA Women's World Cup. The number will jump to 48 in 2026.

Nigeria's goalkeeper, Oyeka Anna Agumanu, and teammate Omo-Love Branch try to stop Germany's Heidi Mohr from scoring in the first round of the 1991 World Cup. Germany went on to win 4–0.

CHAPTER 2

Great Teams

Brazil: 1958–1970

The 1958 World Cup was on TV in many countries. People around the world tuned in to see a 17-year-old star named Pelé. He became the youngest player ever to score a goal in a final game. His team, Brazil, won the World Cup.

This was just the beginning. Brazil's team won three of four World Cup titles from 1958 to 1970. Stars such as Pelé, Hilderaldo Bellini, Nilton Reis dos Santos, and Carlos Alberto were leaders on the field. For 12 years, Brazil was the team to beat at the World Cup.

Pelé

As a young boy, Pelé played soccer by kicking a stuffed sock around his hometown in Brazil. By the time he was 15, he joined the Santos **professional** soccer team. He went on to play with the Brazil national team. He played there for 22 years. During that time, he helped Brazil win three World Cup titles. He is still known as one of the best players of all time. As Carlos Alberto once said, "Playing with Pelé felt like you had God on your side."

Pelé (front) chases after the ball going toward the French goal. Pelé scored three times during this semifinal game at the 1958 World Cup.

West Germany's captain, Lothar Matthëus, dribbles the ball in the 1990 World Cup final.

West Germany: 1974–1990

During the 1970s and 1980s, West Germany had one of the world's best men's teams. They appeared in four out of five World Cup finals. They won the championship in 1974 and 1990.

The West Germans were a strong, single-minded team. In 1974, they came from behind to win the Cup. The Netherlands were favored to win, but West Germany won 2–1. In their 1990 win, West Germany beat Argentina 1–0 in the final game.

Fast Fact!

The common black-and-white pattern on soccer balls was made for the 1970 World Cup. Since the games would be on TV, the ball needed to be easy to see on the screen.

Brazil: 1994–2002

After their run ended in 1970, the Brazil men's team waited 24 years to make it back to the World Cup final. In 1994, they finally made their comeback. Brazil went to three straight World Cup finals from 1994 to 2002.

In 1994, Brazil ended regulation time with a 0–0 tie with Italy. They came through and won in an overtime shoot-out. In 1998, they returned to the World Cup finals but lost to France. In 2002, they won it all again. They beat Germany for their fifth World Cup title.

Ronaldo (second from left) was a star player for Brazil. In 2002, he scored both of Brazil's goals in the final game. The final score was 2–0.

U.S. Women's Team 1991–2019

The first FIFA Women's World Cup was played in 1991. Around the time, the U.S. men's team was having little luck qualifying for the World Cup. The women's team had a chance to win for its country. The team's coach was Anson Dorrance. He built a team of young players. In their first World Cup, the U.S. women outscored the other teams they played 25–5. In 2019, they outscored the other teams 26–3, a record for men's and Women's World Cup.

U.S. player Carin Jennings dribbles up the field during the 1991 semifinals game against Germany.

The 2019 U.S. women's team celebrates their fourth World Cup win.

The FIFA Women's World Cup has been played eight times. The U.S. women's team have won four times. After their 1991 win, they won again in 1999. In the final, the U.S. and China played to a 0–0 tie. That meant a shoot-out would decide the winner. Brandi Chastain, a U.S. forward, scored a penalty kick to win the Cup. They won against Japan in 2015. In 2019, the team beat the Netherlands 2–0.

CHAPTER 3

Amazing Plays

Maradona's Goals

In 1986, Argentina's Diego Maradona scored one of the most famous goals of all time after one of the most questionable goals of all time. Both moments happened during a **quarterfinal** game in the World Cup.

When England's goalie sprinted forward to grab a high-flying ball, Maradona jumped to hit the ball with his head. Maradona got there first. The ball flew into the empty net. It gave Argentina a 1–0 lead. Many people believe that he touched the ball with his hand, which is against the rules, of course. The shot is nicknamed the "Hand of God" goal.

Later in the game, Maradona got the ball on his team's side of the field. He took the ball down the field past five defenders and kicked it past England's goalie once again. The skill he showed was amazing. FIFA later called it the Goal of the Century. Argentina went on to win the game 3–2.

Maradona heads his controversial shot. A replay of the goal proved that he had used his hand. He later admitted it by saying the goal was "a little with the head of Maradona and a little with the hand of God."

Captain Megan Rapinoe takes her penalty kick. Rapinoe won the Golden Boot award. The award is given to the player who scored the most goals in the World Cup.

Rapinoe's World

The 2019 Women's World Cup finals was an important game for the U.S. women's team. So far the U.S. had had a record-breaking tournament. The world was watching to see what the team would do against the Netherlands. The U.S. team couldn't break through the tough **defense** of the Netherlands early on.

There were no goals for either team until the 61st minute. Captain Megan Rapinoe blasted a penalty kick past the goalie to give the U.S. the lead. They never looked back. The U.S. women's team won 2–0. This was their fourth time winning the Cup. Rapinoe won the Golden Ball award as the tournament's best player.

Equal Pay for Equal Play

The U.S. women's team is one of America's best sports teams. They know it, and they want to be paid like it. In 2019, players filed a **lawsuit** against U.S. Soccer. They want to be paid and get the same services as the men's team. Other women's teams around the world want the same. In 2017, Norway agreed to pay the women's and men's team the same amount.

Lloyd's Hat Trick

In 2015, Carli Lloyd of the U.S. team put together the game of a lifetime. She started off scoring her first goal in the third minute of the game. Two minutes later, she knocked the ball into the net again to make the score 2–0.

In minute 16, Lloyd had the ball at midfield—50 yards (45.7 meters) away. She saw Japan's goalie out of position and fired a long shot. It went in! Lloyd had a **hat trick**. It took 15 minutes and 3 seconds—a record in both men's and women's World Cup history. The U.S. women's team went on to win 5–2. They took home their third World Cup title.

Carli Lloyd keeps control of the ball despite the efforts of Japan's Saki Kumagai. Lloyd won FIFA Player of the Year in 2015 and 2016.

Zenga's Goal-Free Streak

Walter Zenga played goalie for Italy in the 1990 World Cup. He wasn't just good that year. He was amazing. Italy won its first five games at the World Cup without giving up a single goal. Zenga was stopping every kick that came at him.

Zenga finally gave up a goal to Argentina in the semifinals. At the end of the game, it was tied 1–1. Then Argentina got a shoot-out goal past Zenga for the win. Italy had given up only two goals in six games of the World Cup. Still, they were out. Argentina later lost to Germany in the final.

Fast Fact!
Goal Line Technology (GLT) uses computer sensors that can tell if a ball has completely crossed the goal line. The World Cup began using it in 2014 for men and in 2015 for women.

Zenga (left) stops an attempted goal during the semifinal game at the 1990 World Cup. Over the course of the tournament, he played 517 minutes before giving up a single goal—a World Cup record.

Glossary

association (uh-SOH-see-ay-shun)—a group of people who are organized to do something together

defense (di-FENS)—the team that tries to stop points from being scored

hat trick (HAT TRIK)—when one player scores three goals in a soccer game

lawsuit (LAW-soot)—a legal action or case brought against a person or group in a court of law

league (LEEG)—a group of sports teams that play against each other

professional (pruh-FESH-uh-nuhl)—making money for doing something others do for fun

qualify (KWAHL-uh-fye)—to reach a level

quarterfinal (KWOR-tur-FINE-al)—the part of a tournament with eight teams remaining; four games are played to decide which four teams go on to the next stage

seeded (SEE-ded)—ranked in number according to their team record for a tournament

Read More

Doeden, Matt. *The World Cup: Soccer's Global Championship*. Minneapolis: Millbrook Press, 2018.

Peterson, Megan Cooley. *Wacky Soccer Trivia: Fun Facts for Every Fan*. North Mankato, MN: Capstone Press, 2019.

Terrell, Brandon. *Soccer Showdown: U.S. Women's Stunning 1999 World Cup Win*. North Mankato, MN: Capstone Press, 2019.

Internet Sites

FIFA Grassroots Soccer
grassroots.fifa.com/en/for-kids.html

Sports Illustrated Kids Soccer
www.sikids.com/soccer

World History of Soccer
www.socialstudiesforkids.com/articles/sports/soccer_worldcuphistory.htm

Index

Argentina, 17, 22, 28
    Maradona, Diego, 22
awards, 4, 25

Brazil, 10, 14, 18
    Alberto, Carlos, 14
    Bellini, Hilderaldo, 14
    Pelé, 14
    Reis dos Santos, Nilton, 14

China, 12, 21
    Ma Li, 12

England, 22

Fédération Internationale de Football Association (FIFA), 6, 8, 12, 20, 22
France, 4, 6, 18
    Hernandez, Lucas, 4
    Mbappé, Kylian, 4

Germany, 18, 28
Goal Line Technology, 28

hat tricks, 27

Italy
    Zenga, Walter, 28

Japan, 21, 27

Netherlands, the, 6, 17, 21, 25
Norway, 25

pay, 25
Pickles, 6

qualifying, 12

records, 20, 27

soccer balls, 17
Spain, 6
stages, 10
stars, 10
Summer Olympics, 8

United States, 10, 12, 20–21, 25, 27
    Chastain, Brandi, 21
    Dorrance, Anson, 20
    Lloyd, Carli, 27
    Rapinoe, Megan, 25

West Germany, 17
World Cup trophy, 6